CW00821649

Introduction

The 1960s scooter scene was always going to be a hard act to follow. Things didn't get off to a good start in the 70s when, in the spring of 1971, Innocenti announced that Lambretta production would cease with immediate effect. These were changing times and as the scooter slowly fell out of favour as a daily commuter vehicle its days seemed numbered. Ownership now belonged to the younger generation, but it had become fragmented and dispersed across the country. The north of England would be regarded as the mainstay with odd pockets of owners surviving in other areas. The problem was, there was nothing linking them together.

There were those determined to unite scooterists once again and make them a strong force, but it was a unique set of circumstances that eventually became the catalyst in making it all happen. A film about mods, bands influenced by the movement, and reports in the music press of a revival all stirred up interest. Now those who had stuck with scooters through the underground years were reinforced by a tidal wave of young teenagers keen to be part of the latest fashion uprising.

Suddenly scooters were in vogue once again but this time it was different; the scooter was no longer just a form of transport but one of expression. Along with it came the impending trouble fuelled by the media frenzy, overhyping the situation. Though the mod revival was short-lived, it had generated a new breed of scooter owners. The parkas would soon be ditched but the scooters would stay and as the decade came to an end something special was happening to help lay the perfect foundation for the scooter scene to explode into the 1980s.

PICTURE CREDITS AND THANKS

Thomas Crinigan, Chas de Lacy, Peter Ham, Mike Hayman, Norrie Kerr, Nigel Lowe, Iggy Mycock, Walter Nelson-Aylott, Dave Omerod, Frank Osgerby, Richard Oswald, Steve Saffin, Mark Sargeant, Gloria Saunders, Alan Smith, Jim Stretton, Terry Walton, Graham Wallace, John Webster, Richard Wilfang, Rob Williams, Paul Wood and the team at Mortons Archive

Author: Stuart Owen
Design: Burda Druck India Pvt. Ltd.
Publisher: Steve O'Hara
Published by: Mortons Media Group Ltd, Media Centre, Morton Way, Horncastle, Lincolnshire LN9 6JR
Tel. 01507 529529
Printed by: William Gibbons and Sons, Wolverhampton

ISBN: 978-1-911639-96-1

16-year-old John Webster at the start of his long affiliation with the Lambretta

Isle of Man

SCOOTER HOLIDAY WEEK

Photograph by courtesy of W. H. Heaps.

1970

Pete Meads of Luton Lambretta Club ready to go at the Isle of Man scooter week 1970

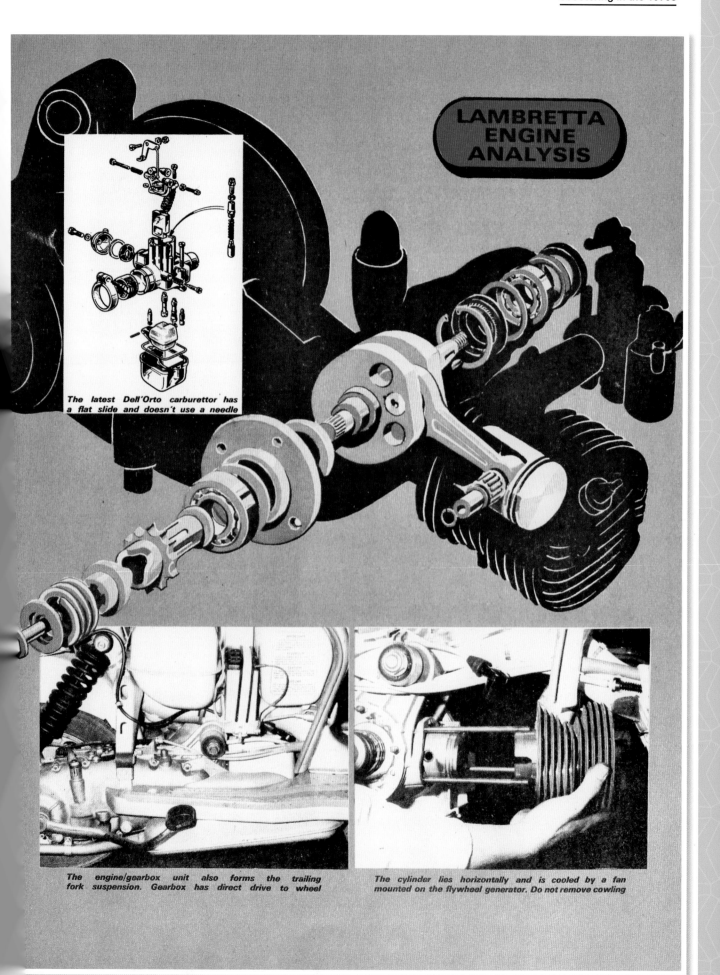

LAMBRETTA ENGINE ANALYSIS

The latest Dell'Orto carburettor has a flat slide and doesn't use a needle

The engine/gearbox unit also forms the trailing fork suspension. Gearbox has direct drive to wheel

The cylinder lies horizontally and is cooled by a fan mounted on the flywheel generator. Do not remove cowling

3

"SWINGERS" WIN LAMBRETTAS

Luna Line Lambrettas Offered As Star Prize In Nationwide Contest

More than 2,000 teenaged pop fans packed out the Top Rank Suite in
Croydon last week to watch the finals of a nationwide competition
in which two Luna Line Lambrettas were offered as the first prize.

Sponsored by the cosmetic firm 'Sylvakleer', heats for the "Swingers
Contest" had taken place at Top Rank ballrooms all over the country
and, watched by hundreds of fellow teenagers, the mainly 16-18 year old
contestants entered in couples to try their luck at answering questions
on any one of five possible subjects: Sport; Health, Fashion & Beauty;
TV & Films; General Knowledge; or The Pop Scene.

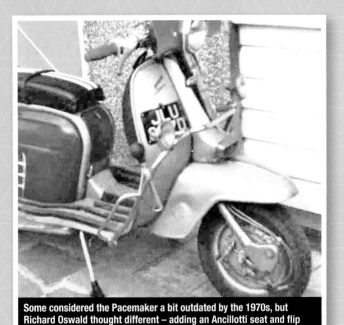

Some considered the Pacemaker a bit outdated by the 1970s, but
Richard Oswald thought different – adding an Ancillotti seat and flip
over backrest

LAMBRETTA RE-INTRODUCE MOST POPULAR SCOOTER

EVER MARKETED IN UK
Li 150 at Outdoor Life and Holiday Show

The most popular scooter ever marketed by Lambretta
Concessionaires,Ltd., – the Li 150 – is being
re-introduced into the U.K. at the Outdoor Life and
Holiday Show at Olympia (Jan 6 – 16) on Stand 1/124.
At a recommended retail price of £179.19.0d., inc.P.T.,
it is only £9.19.0d. more than when it was sold here
seven years ago!

Said Mr.Maurice Knight, Group Sales Manager: "Demand
for this particular Lambretta model never waned and was
reflected to a considerable extent in the second-hand
market for which, now, there is a dearth of machines
generally.   As a result, there is bound to be a ready

With Lambretta supplies exhausted due to the problems in Italy, Lambretta
Concessionaires looked to the Serveta to help solve the problem

148·59·111

CURVY, LOVABLE LAMBRETTA — the new beauty from
Spain with a figure like this what more could a guy want !

148 cc
59 mph   LI 150
111 mpg

LI 150 £214.50 Recommended Retail Price inc. P.T.
SX 200 £259.50 Recommended Retail Price inc. P.T.

Please send me the rest of Lambretta's vital statistics.

Name _____

Address _____

_____

Age if under 17 _____   MCM7

Suzuki (G.B.) Ltd., 87 Beddington Lane, Croydon, CRO 4TD.

SPORTS SHOW SPECIAL!

JANUARY 1971   2/6d

MOTORCYCLE
SCOOTER & THREE-WHEELER
MECHANICS
LARGEST SALE

FREE 5⁄-
TICKET !

see offer inside
and full preview

SEE THEM AT THE SHOW !

● **Start first time** ● **Suzuki 250 engine analysis**
● **Scooter tune for sport** ● **Metisse 8-valve test**

The scooter market's decline in the 1970s was evident in the magazines that supported it, either going out of business or being tacked on to motorcycle publications

Lambretta Concessionaires Ltd

Lambretta House Purley Way Croydon
CR9 4HD England Phone: 01 686 2499
Telex: 21138 Cables: Lambretta Croydon

TO ALL LAMBRETTA DEALERS.   No. 7/71.

LAMBRETTA DELIVERIES.

Everyone must be aware of the current scooter and motor cycle boom.
Our sales forecasts have been far exceeded and our production
capacity for some models is already exhausted.

The problems of strike, wage claims and other industrial difficul-
ties, as well as the increased lead times for raw materials, lead
us to inform you that the delivery position obtains as follows :-

> GP.200   —   no more orders can be
>   accepted until after the
>   factory holiday shut-down
>   in August.
>
> Spanish LI.150   —   no more orders for delivery
>   before July. However, limited
>   supplies will be available
>   from July onwards. It is
>   necessary to increase immedi-
>   ately the recommended retail
>   price. This includes orders
>   at present outstanding.

The new recommended retail price will be as follows :-

> £142.93 plus £42.04 purchase tax = £184.97
>
> Main Dealer margin C.O.D. Terms = £29. 40

> GP.150   —   Delays may occur on specific
>   colour ranges but stock
> GP.125   available.
>
> VEGA   —   all available ex-stock.
> COMETA   —   Limited supplies only.
>   Colours Apple Green & Ochre.

We give this information to our Dealers so that they are fully in
the picture in regard to the production and supply problems which
are at present prevailing.

                                                    May, 1971.

tune it !

for Lambretta Series 2, slimstyle and Grand Prix models.

Our stage 4 tuning is the ideal. On a mechanically sound engine the admitted extra stress if using the performance consistently will have negligable reduction in the life of the unit. Tuning should not be entertained to obtain performance lost to below standard output, through incorrect, or insufficient maintenance, the worst offender points - timing. If your Lambretta is rough, spend the money getting it right, then have the tuning to get above standard acceleration and speed.

The ultimate is with a Large Bore Clubman exhaust, and a larger carburettor, but electronic tests with a stage 4 tune on a standard carburettor and exhaust gave a genuine 6 miles an hour on top speed, and greatly improved acceleration. With a racing Large Bore Clubman exhaust and 30mm carburettor, a Grand Prix 200 with full tunework has exceeded a genuine - not tuned speedometer - 86 miles an hour.

STAGE 4 TUNE We require barrel, piston, head, induction manifold.

The components are immersed in a non corrosive cleaning agent, checked for wear and if within tolerances the following effected. Exhaust port raised, profiled and finished. Transfer ports modified, and blended. Induction port and manifold matched & polished. Cylinder head skimmed, shaped and polished. (200cc models pre number 8000 with central squish head are advised to replace it with side squish type, additional £2.50).

150cc ..... £9.00   190cc ..... £8.50   175cc £7.50
200cc ..... £7.00   225cc £6.50

Sending by post, pack carefully. For return registered post, send further 85p.

...mphasis had shifted to tuning and performance, particularly with ...ambretta

The selection of carburettor choices became even bigger

There was still of course the Wal Phillips fuel injector for Vespa and Lambretta owners who wanted that instant bolt-on power boost

WAL PHILLIPS (MOTOR CYCLES) **LTD.**

CAR AND MOTORCYCLE
SPECIALIST

114 & 116 NEW KENT ROAD
LONDON   S.E.1
Telephone : 01-703-6980

WAL PHILLIPS FUEL INJECTORS (PATENTED)

WAL PHILLIPS FUEL INJECTORS
130 NORTH STREET ROMFORD, ESSEX·
ROMFORD 61287

Dear Sir

Please send £1.30 to
cover jet assemblies and p.p.
and oblige
Yours faithfully
Wal Phillips

LAMBRETTA NEWSLETTER AF/L/5.72.

Our 1971 Newsletters helped to stop many wild rumours as to the future of the Lambretta, carrying then up to date information. The situations now seems stable, as follows.

Innocenti, the Italian designers and manufacturers, ceased production of the Lambretta scooter early in 1971, though considerable numbers of machines completed, and en route maintained supplies for many months, and even now we hear of the occasional machine still unsold in a dealers showroom.

Over ten years ago a Spanish concern set up Lambretta scooter production under licence, as exceptionally harsh import restrictions made it impractical to buy from Italy. Selling only in Spain, it was essential to absorb tooling costs over a set number of units made, and with the relatively small annual sales, a model was retained as 'current' sometimes years after a later version was available from Italy. There was also a slight divergence of evolution, many of the Spanish parts not interchangeable with the Italian models, though

Arthur Francis Limited issues a newsletter to reassure owners that it will continue to stock spares to keep Lambrettas on the road despite production stopping at the Innocenti factory

Starting at the crankshaft, the two holes in the flywheel can be filled with aluminium or cork plugs held by Araldite

SOUPER SCOOTER

Build a better 'bretta with this tuning advice from Rafferty Newman's racing shop

The ports in the barrel may be modified, as described in text below. Make sure that the transfer ports match cutaways on piston

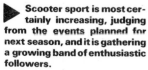

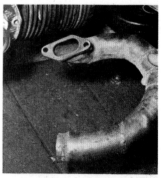

There is no special exhaust pipe available, but one can easily be made up for use with silencer — see below

Scooter sport is most certainly increasing, judging from the events planned for next season, and it is gathering a growing band of enthusiastic followers.

Machines vary from the virtually standard to the full-blown racing variety like the outfits pictured above.

Down at the Rafferty Newman shop in West Street, Fareham, where they build their own racers and do a good job making other people's scooters go quicker, Les Rafferty showed us how he builds up a racing Lambretta.

To start, you don't need to take the motor out of the frame

—it can be stripped *in situ*. Les started on a 200 which had had the crankshaft removed. The gearbox and clutch were still *virgo intacto*, as the saying goes.

The best crankshaft to use is the GP-type—it has a stronger conrod and the taper is better for the later type flywheel.

The shaft web is the full circle type, with a couple of holes in it. These can be filled up to reduce crankcase volume, and Les uses cork discs made from bottle corks from the chemist. Aluminium plugs could also be made; in either case, they are stuck in with Araldite.

When you fit the nearside

crankcase cover or bearing housing, don't fit the gasket. This allows the housing to go further into the case and reduces volume still more. Use non-setting jointing compound to keep the seal.

The next step is for racers only. The flywheel can be cut down substantially—see photograph above—and the coils removed from the stator, leaving the contact breaker unit. Rafferty Newman will do this for you if you give them the flywheel and some money.

Ignition is then supplied from a battery, through a coil to the contact breakers.

The barrel can be altered fairly drastically by opening the ports and by overboring to a larger size. The ports go like this: exhaust—raised 2.5 mm, sideways 1 mm each way; transfer—just make sure they both open at the same time; intake—lower by 2 mm, widen by 3 mm on right-hand side (offside).

overbored

Bore conversions, complete with pistons will give the following increases: 150–175 cc, 175–200 cc, 200–225 cc, and Rafferty Newman can supply special Dykes pistons for these and the standard 200.

48

Jim Stretton, having just purchased a brand new Lambretta GP 200, immediately took it racing as the first full season of a British scooter championship took hold

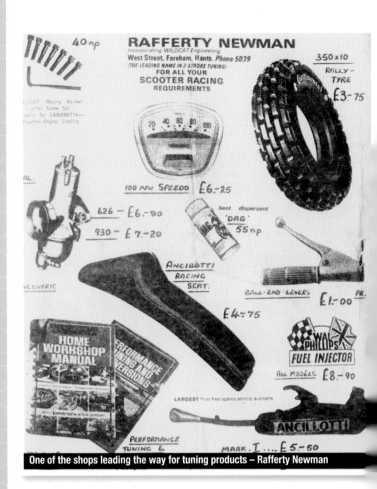

One of the shops leading the way for tuning products – Rafferty Newman

A sad reflection of how the Lambretta was no longer the biggest player in the two-wheeled market – looking lost in a sea of motorcycles at a show

What goes up…

…Must come down. Scooter scrambling at an old disused quarry on a modified Lambretta

MOTOR SPORT By MATT SHELLEY
Girl friend races to scooter win

246cc scooter faster than 1,300cc sidecar

SCOOTER WORLD
AND LIGHTWEIGHT MOTORCYCLE

DECEMBER 1972

In this issue

Too much oil
—a warning

New Twisty
Sprint at
Curborough

Nick Barnes
and Kent
Scooter Mart

GAL 43J

Scooter World magazine had served well since the mid-1950s but by the early 1970s was no longer financially viable

Peter Ham takes a rest before preparing to go out on his 90mph+ Lambretta sprinter

The legendary Fred Willingham as he breaks the 14-second barrier on his modified Lambretta, the first person to ever do so

Lambretta series one machines using a mix of old and new components to make them ideal scramblers

Record Holder
112 mph 180 kph

UP U2

Fred's answer to the critics who doubted he could make a Lambretta go that fast

A neatly turned out SX 200 still going strong into the 1970s

Sometimes not always easy to get it right

The art of drifting is a hard skill to acquire on a scooter

Piaggio's answer to keeping Vespa sales going in the 1970s: the Rally 200

Not only the most powerful Vespa ever built but now with electronic ignition

VESPA RALLY 200

ELECTRONIC IGNITION - "DUCATI" TYPE

1) Main advantages.

In comparison with the traditional ignition, both with a magneto and with a battery, the electronic ignition "with discharge of condenser" presents some advantages of electric and mechanic nature, of which we resume the principal ones:

A) Advantages of electric nature.

The particular characteristic of the H.T. discharge with electronic ignition in comparison with the traditional ignitions, is essentially that to produce a higher tension peak reached in a very short time and with a shorter total length of the discharge itself.

It follows:

- Engine regular running also with dirty spark-plugs or with electrode gap not correct.

- Better starting facility with cold engine.

- Higher life of the spark plugs because of a smaller electrodes wear

- Less possibilities of arc on spark-plug.

B) Mechanic advantages.

The absence of the parts exposed to the wear as the contact breaker, cam unit allows:

- Unalterability, during the time, of the ignition advance.

- Insensibility to the atmospheric agents.

- Regular engine running also to the high speeds.

- Certain ignition runnig also after large periods when the vehicle is not used.

To these advantages prevalently functional it can be added, not less important, that of an almost total absence of maintenance.

PIAGGIO

BY - Royspeed

A LIMITED AMOUNT OF CAREFULLY PREPARED MACHINES WITH THE FOLLOWING SPECIFICATION ARE BEING OFFERED FOR THE 1971 SEASON

TRANSISTORISED IGNITION

12 VOLT LIGHTING

FULL RACE TUNED BARREL & PISTON AT 200cc

(AS USED BY RON MOSS)

5 SPEED GEARBOX (available shortly)

30 mm DEL'ORTO CARBURETTOR

(fitted with larger pulley wheel for better control)

SPECIAL 44mm ROYSPEED EXHAUST SYSTEM

DOUBLE ENGINE MOUNTS WITH HEAT DEFLECTORS

FIBRE-GLASS FRONT WING & SIDE PANELS

FINISHED IN ALL WHITE WITH SIGNWRITTEN

PANELS ROYSPEED & CUSTOMERS NAME

ALL THE ABOVE SPECIFICATION
WITH NEW G.P. AT AN
INCLUSIVE PRICE

£299

ORDERS NOW
TAKEN

FIRST COME
FIRST SERVED

ROY of Hornchurch (Enterprises) Ltd.

35 HIGH STREET, HORNCHURCH, ESSEX.
PLEASE SEND FOR FURTHER INFORMATION

PIAGGIO

Vespa

rally

Not yet legal to drive on the road, but that didn't bother Rob Williams who proudly poses on his skelly

What do you do when buying a brand New Jet 200? Simply put your own mark on it

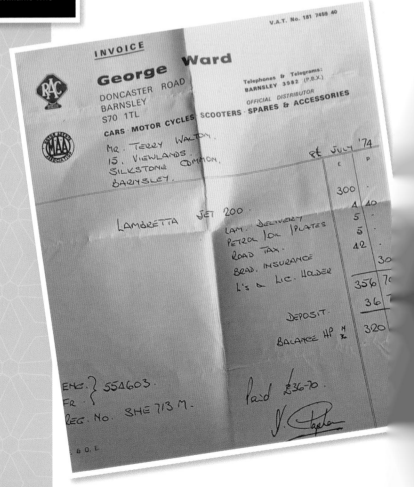

Being proud of your club and where you were from became the new fashion, displayed on many a backrest

The Lambretta series two wasn't the ideal candidate to be a race scooter – unless you had reed valve induction fitted. This Lambretta was one of the first to do so

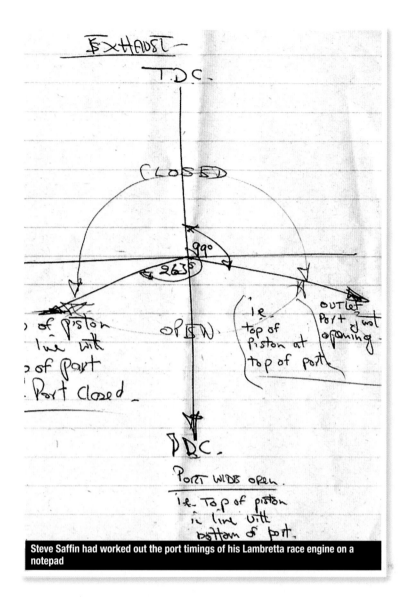

EXHAUST –

T.D.C.

CLOSED

99°

263°

OPEN

... of piston
... line with
... of port
... Port closed.

'ie
top of
piston at
top of port

outlet
port is not
opening.

B.D.C.

PORT WIDE OPEN.
ie. Top of piston
is line with
bottom of port.

Steve Saffin had worked out the port timings of his Lambretta race engine on a notepad

Putting those calculations to the test at Barbon Manor Park hill climb

As the decade progressed the mod scooter look once again became fashionable

Richard Wilfang sitting on his group four Lambretta, learning the trade. He would later become British champion

THE 1975 SCOOTER LAP RECORDS CHART

Grouped Classes	Up to 104cc	Up to 129cc	Up to 158cc	Up to 209cc	158cc Specs	300cc Specs	Combinations
Ballaugh 2.7 miles Last used 1973	J.Collins 20/6/73 3m 21.2s 48.31 mph	A.Smith 20/8/73 3m 2.0s 53.39 mph	N.Burgess 20/8/73 2m 31s 56.83 mph	R.Kemp 20/6/73 2m 49.0s 60.74 mph	N.Burgess 20/6/73 2m 56.4s 57.05 mph	D.May 20/6/73 2m 36.8s 61.98 mph	Frost/Flanagan 20/6/73 3m 0.2s 53.96 mph
Castle Combe 1.84 miles Last used 1972	C.Hart 21/8/71 1m 53.5s 58.4 mph △	T.Sharp 21/10/72 1m 42.5s 64.6 mph	A.Jupp 21/10/72 1m 41.0s 65.6 mph	Frost/Hearn 21/10/72 1m 33.8s 70.8 mph	R.Myers 21/10/72 1m 38.0s 67.6 mph	C.Armett 5/5/71 1m 30.7s 73.03 mph	Frost/Flanagan 21/10/72 1m 42.0s 64.9 mph
Jurby 1.28 miles ✱	I. Frankland 1m 42.0s 45.17mph	T.Frankland 1m 34.5s 48.76 mph	D.Webster 1m 34.4s 48.81 mph	D.Willfang 1m 24.6s 54.46 mph	D.Webster 1m 35.4s 48.30 mph	D.Willfang 1m 22.8s 55.65 mph	Stevens/Myers 1m 30.4s 50.97
Cadwell Park Club Circuit 1.5 miles	C.Hart 23/8/75 1m 44.0s 51.92 mph ✱	J.Ronald 23/8/75 1m 37.0s 55.67 mph ✱	D.Webster 23/8/75 1m 32.2s 58.57 mph ✱	M.Hayman 23/8/75 1m 28.45s 61.03 mph ✱	D.Webster 23/8/75 1m 33.0s 58.06 mph ✱	T.Pead 1/6/74 1m 26.2s 62.64 mph	Green/McGee 31/8/74 1m 37.4s 55.44 mph
Cadwell Park Full Circuit 2.25 miles Last used 1973	G.Pearce 2/9/73 2m 35.9s 51.95 mph	T.Sharp 2/9/73 2m 19.3s 58.14 mph	N.Burgess 2/9/73 2m 19.2s 58.18 mph	D.May 2/9/73 2m 8.2s 63.18 mph	G.Oliver 2/9/73 2m 14.9s 60.04 mph	B.Metcalf 2/9/73 2m 5.9s 64.33 mph	Frost/Flanagan 2/9/73 2m 26.5s 55.29 mph
Croft 1.75 miles	C.Hart 14/9/74 1m 53.5s 55.50 mph	J.Ronald 4/8/73 1m 47.5s 58.60 mph	A.Lord 14/9/74 1m 42.6s 61.40 mph	D.May 14/9/74 1m 36.4s 65.35 mph	A.Lord 14/9/74 1m 42.3s 61.58 mph	R.Kemp 14/9/74 1m 38.1s 65.42mph	Wilcock/Tooley 14/9/74 1m 48.1s 58.28 mph
Llandow 1.00 mile	C.Hart 7/9/75 55.25s 65.21 mph	T.Frankland 7/6/75 53.8s 66.91 mph ✱	D.Webster 7/6/75 51.23s 70.31 mph ✱	G.Stephens 7/6/75 49.0s 73.47 mph ✱	D.Webster 7/6/75 50.65s 71.14 mph ✱	M.Hayman 7/6/75 48.8s 73.77 mph	Crickmore/Hinsley & Green/McGee 7/6/75 54.1s 66.54 mph ✱
Longridge 0.42 miles Last used 1972	Hinchcliffe 6/8/72 39.8s 38.6 mph △	P.Chapman 6/8/72 37.0s 40.8 mph	K.Reilly 6/8/72 36.7s 42.4 mph	M.Redfern 6/8/72 35.0s 43.3 mph	R.Myers 6/8/72 35.9s 41.0 mph	Bexon/Louth 6/8/72 35.0s 43.3 mph	Walsh/McGee 6/8/72 36.8s 41.1 mph
Lydden Hill 1.00 mile	C.Hart 4/10/75 1m 03.0s 57.14 mph ✱	T.Sharp 30/9/72 1m 2.65s 57.5 mph	D.Webster 28/10/74 53.6s 60.40 mph	Pead/May 27/7 & 26/10 57.2s /74 62.93 mph	R.Myers 4/11/72 58.0s 62.1 mph	D.Willfang 4/10/75 56.4s 63.82 mph ✱	Green/McGee 26/10/74 1m 00.7s 59.31 mph
Mallory Park Full Circuit 1.35 miles Last used 1970	C.Hart 25/10/70 1m 29.4s 53.7 mph △	N.Barnes 31/5/70 1m 17.2s 62.3 mph	M.Dawson 31/5/70 1m 14.4s 64.8 mph	B.Moss 25/10/70 1m 10.5s 68.0 mph	Class not formed	C.Armett 25/10/70 1m 9.5s 68.9 mph	Burnhill/Mansfield 31/5/70 1m 21.0s 59.5 mph
Mallory Park Club Circuit 1.00 mile Last used 1971	C.Hart 18/7/71 58.4s 61.7 mph	T.Sharp 18/7/71 54.2s 66.4 mph	D.Tooley 18/7/71 53.4s 67.4 mph	R.Moss 18/7/71 49.6s 72.7 mph	R.Moss 18/7/71 52.1s 69.0 mph	C.Armett 6/6/71 48.0s 75.0 mph	Moorhouse/Southern 18/7/71 55.6s 64.6 mph
Snetterton Full Circuit 2.71 miles Last used 1973	J.Ronald 31/10/71 2m 43.6s 59.63 mph △	N.Ronald 31/10/71 2m 31.8s 64.27 mph	N.Frost 11/11/73 2m 24.0s 67.75 mph	N.Frost 11/11/73 2m 15.5s 72.00 mph	G.Pearce 11/11/73 2m 28.2s 65.82 mph	C.Armett 31/10/71 2m 13.6s 73.02 mph	Hycock/Marchant 11/11/73 2m 35.0s 62.94 mph
Snetterton Club Circuit 1.917 miles ✱	C.Hart 15/3/75 2m 10.1s 53.04 mph	T.Frankland 15/3/75 1m 59.6s 57.70 mph	S.Ives 15/3/75 1m 58.9s 58.04 mph	D.May 15/3/75 1m 49.4s 63.08 mph	M.Cable 11/3/75 1m 57.1s 58.93 mph	D.Willfang 15/3/75 1m 47.7s 64.07 mph	Crickmore/Hinsley 15/3/75 1m 59.6s 57.70 mph
Thruxton 2.35 miles Last used 1970	C.Hart 15/3/70 2m 35.1s 54.6 mph	N.Barnes 15/3/70 2m 22.4s 59.4 mph	M.Dawson 15/3/70 2m 16.3s 61.2 mph	R.Moss 15/3/70 2m 5.5s 67.50 mph	Class not formed	C.Armett 15/3/70 2m 8.8s 65.7 mph	Frost/Flanagan 15/3/70 2m 31.5s 55.4 mph

Records standing as at 1st January 1976. ✱Indicates record set in 1975. △Indicates a capacity below 77cc. Table up-dated by Nigel Orr on behalf of the London Area Scooter Clubs Association, originally compiled and published by Club & Circuit Magazine. Produced for LASCA by C & C Productions and printed by Peter J. Mitchell Ltd., South Croydon.

LONDON AREA SCOOTER CLUBS ASSOCIATION

Chairman: Mr A M Hillman
234 Kent House Road, Beckenham, Kent, BR3 1JN.

The water splash at the Isle of Man in the mid-1970s, Vespa style

On a Lambretta

Or a scooter sidecar outfit

Vic Saunders looking cool next to his Wildcat TV 175

espas lined up before the start of the tour of Wales

Some would complete the tour in resounding success…

…others were not so lucky as the aftermath of this crash shows. The owner was put in hospital with a broken arm

Off-road trials would remain a popular form of scooter sport and the agile small frame Vespa was the ideal machine to compete on

while in Italy the handlebars got bigger and wider

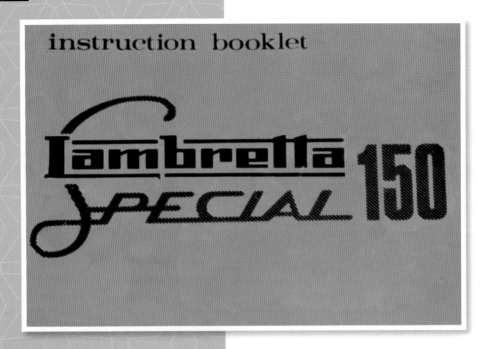

A nicely prepared and championship-winning group six Lambretta, held upright by the obligatory piece of wood

Scooter record may be illegal

DICK WILLFANG (200 Lambretta) set a new record for scooters at Lydden Circuit, Kent, on Saturday, with 56.40s for the mile lap. He clipped half a second of his previous best.

But the big query is will the time stand? It came in a re-run which was later held to be il-legal under the regulations. This prevented Dick from scor-ing four wins, two in the up to 209cc, and the first of the 209 standards and specials to 300.

PROVISIONAL RESULTS

First to 104cc: 1 C Hart (96 Vespa), 2 I Frankland (100 Vespa), 3 R Owen (75 Lambretta). **Second up to 104cc:** 1 Hart, 2 I Frankland, 3 R Aylmer (100 Vespa).

First to 129cc: 1 T Frankland (125 Vespa), 2 V Dachtler (125 Lambretta), 3 C Watson (125 Lambretta). Second race — same placings.

First to 158cc: 1 S Ives (150 Lambretta), 2 C Charnley (150 Lambretta), 3 S Collett (148 Lambret-ta). **Second to 158cc:** 1 D Webster (150 Lambretta), 2 Ives, 3 P Bean (150 Lambretta).

First 209cc: 1 Dick Willfang (200 Lambretta), 2 M Hayman (200 Lambretta), 3 P Kenchington (200 Lambretta). **Second 209cc:** 1 Willfang, 2 Kenchington, 3 T Pead (198 Lambret-ta).

First to 158cc specials: 1 D Webster (151 Lambretta), 2 B Passingham (150 Lambretta), 3 G Oliver (150 Lambret-ta). **Second 158cc specials:** 1 S Ives (150 Lambretta), 2 Oliver, 3 J East (150 Lambretta).

Standards over 209cc and sp to 300cc: 1 Dick Willfan Lambretta), 2 Pead (204 Lamb Hayman.

First combinations to 322c Browning/K Barnes (225 Lamb A Crickmore/P Hinsley (198 ta), 3 D Dalton/J Jubb (225 La **Second combo:** 1 Brow Crickmore, 3 A Smith/P Sm Lambretta).

A nicely prepared special. The owner was soon to become one of the biggest names in the scene, none other than Dave Webster

e grid in the mid-1970s was always full of nicely presented Lambrettas, dly surprising as most of them were only a few years old

Coasting around to the start line at Cadwell Park, each class was hugely contested

Mycock flat out at the Doune hill climb on his 150cc special – ng he was still competitive on two wheels despite switching to ar racing

Making a scooter go fast was one thing but stopping it was another. Mike Hayman came up with the answer – fitting a hydraulic disc brake to the Lambretta

AMAL *Sales Announcement* *No. 11*

Mark 2 Range of Amal Concentric Carburetors

Developed from the well-known Mark 1 Amal Concentric, the Mark 2 range has been designed to meet the exacting performance rèquirements of modern motorcycles. It has also been given the functional styling currently popular among riders world-wide.

The Mark 2 range is available in three body sizes, giving an option of ten bore diameters from 22 to 40 mm. A number of extra features are incorporated:

★ The smoothly contoured tract shape of the air intake tube tapers concentrically straight into the carburetor bore, giving improved air flow and greater engine power output.

★ The cold-starting mixture-enrichment device is operated by a lever mounted directly on the carburetor body. An alternative arrangement with cable control from the handlebar, or elsewhere on the machine is also available (as illustrated on this page).

★ The carburetor is designed for flexible mounting, giving excellent insulation from vibration on modern high-speed high-performance engines.

★ The screw-off top to the mixing chamber allows quick and easy servicing and tuning.

★ Two float-chamber vent tubes mounted high up on the carburetor body prevent fuel spillage under extreme conditions.

★ To achieve a truly light-weight carburetor, the body and other component parts are precision diecast in aluminium alloy.

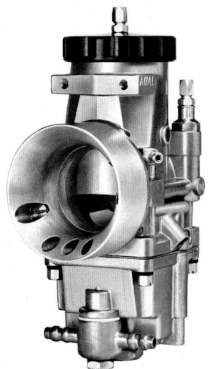

Obtainable from

dealer

Amal · Holdford Road · Birmingham · England · B6 7ES

a subsidiary of IMI

☎ 021-356 4801   Telegrams: 'Amalcarb Phone Birmingham'   Telex: Bircom G 338024—begin all messages 'Amal'

Working in the paddock on your scooter was much easier if you had an old orange box lying around

Also making a name for himself and soon to be Dave Webster's business partner, on the right, Norrie Kerr

Hardly a Formula One paddock but scooter racers were made of hard stuff and put up with the conditions they faced

Transporting their scooters by whatever means necessary

Away from racing, customising scooters was a way of creating your own identity and the scene was ready to explode

There was a growing club culture with club members who wanted their scooters to look the best

The club scene was certainly gaining momentum up the north end of the country

From Lancashire to Yorkshire, the scooter scene remained strong

TWO WHEELS '77

The Annual Festival of Scootering

On the other hand, backrests would be decorated with what looked like the inside contents of a car

This was the beginning of major custom paint schemes as murals began gracing panel work

The Vespa was the only scooter left in production but the design needed a major overhaul

That would come by way of a completely new look, the P range

The Vespa PX 125, ready to take Piaggio into the future

vespa P200E

STOP PRESS

P 200E was the most powerful Vespa to date

Opposite, we print with pleasure, the SCOOP OF THE YEAR as regards scootering in the United Kingdom. The Lambretta-looking Vespa which has new styling, new 90-type front suspension, new gear-change system, should be on show and we hope available in 1978. Although our copy is not the best reproduction, you will see a new style headlamp assembly, new style mudguard, new style side panels, new style seat, and loads of little improvements. The engine is an Electronic 200 and is a three-port two stroke. The Spanish version shown, is available as a six-volt 50 watt or twelve-volt 80 watt. One noticeable characteristic is the very square mudguard and horn casting that is reminiscent of many a good-looking Lambretta. Our S. & S. correspondent informs us that the engine layout has had some considerable changes, notably on the kick-start side, as shown in our photo. We are proud to be the first to show this new Vespa to scooterists in the U. K., and rightly so. This is indeed a scoop brought to you by Scooter & Scooterist, the first with the scoops-the people in the know.

News of its launch in the UK came curtesy of Scooter and Scooterist magazine produced by Norrie Kerr, much to the annoyance of Piaggio

The new line Vespa all squared off at the front

Basic tools were all that was needed, so assured was Piaggio of its scooters' reliability

September 1977

Lambretta

Grand Prix 150
Colours: white,
autumn sky, tangerine

£349.95 recommended retail price
(£388.45 inc. delivery & V.A.T.)

Grand Prix 200
Delivery: Spring 1978

£399.95 recommended retail price
(£442.45 inc. delivery & V.A.T.)

SPECIAL INTRODUCTORY OFFER
(while stocks last)

Lambretta Li 150
Colour: cream

£299.95 recommended retail price

Lambretta SX 200
Colour: tangerine

£399.95 recommended retail price

The R.R. Prices on the Li 150 and SX 200 include delivery
and V.A.T.

ACCESSORIES

A full range of genuine Lambretta accessories will be available from your local agent.
This will include front and rear crash bars, windscreen, inside legshield bag, rear carriers, spare wheel, mudflap, front carrier, Lambretta jacket and backrest.

At the same time, thanks to Scooters India Limited, the Lambretta Grand Prix would be reintroduced back into the UK market

Lambretta

GRAND PRIX 150

Maximum speed	62.4 mph.
	55 ½m 21.6 secs.
Power (Din bhp)	9.27 bhp
Fuel consumption	86.2 mpg
Engine	Air cooled 2 stroke single cylinder
	148 cc
	57 x 58 mm
Compression ratio	8.25 to 1
	Petrol/oil mixture 25 to 1
Transmission	4 speed constant mesh.
	Chain drive in oil bath.
	Multi disc in oil bath.
Tank capacity	1.78 Gallons (8.1 litres)
Frame	Tubular steel chassis.
Wheelbase	5.8 in (1292 mm)
Max width	70.8 in (1800 mm)
Max height	26.8 in (660 mm)
Seat height	39.8 in (1012 mm)
	30.39 in (772 mm)
	FRONT: trailing links with helical springs.
	REAR: swinging crankcase and shock absorber unit.
Brakes	Drum
Kerb weight	264 lbs
Tyres	3.50 x 10

Lambretta has become a legend in its own lifetime. The latest genuine Grand Prix 150 models, continue the famous tradition.

Exceptionally low running costs against any car, light handling, manoeuverability and ease of parking, make the Grand Prix 150 a commuting favourite. It's fun and fashionable.

Think Grand Prix 150 Lambretta. The in machine.

Specifications and colours of all models are liable to change without prior notice. Please contact your Lambretta dealer before purchasing.

Genuine **Lambretta**

LAMBRETTA Sole UK Concessionaires Two Four Accessories Limited, 53 Clapham Common Southside, London SW4 9BU.

Whether or not the Lambretta could take on the might of the Vespa after its seven-year absence was the question now being asked

The new Lambretta GP minus panel stripes – something was definitely missing

The Vespa was advertised as the ideal machine for a city commuter…

…whereas the Lambretta was more daring and fun related or so they wanted the public to believe

scooters

Lambretta
SERVETA

*I vantaggi più importanti li troverete nella varietà dei modelli
tutti in linee della massima attualità; una meccanica
tra le più moderne; colori armoniosi e uso estremamente
economico.*

*Concepiti in modo particolare per soddisfare le esigenze
più raffinate, per il loro facile mantenimento, la
velocità, la solidità, l'eleganza e la sicurezza.*

*Essi offrono una semplicità di trasporto, una facilità di
parcheggio, la possibilità di escursioni al mare, in
montagna ecc...*

LAMBRETTA LO SCOOTER CHE DURA DI PIU'

SCOOTERLINEA 125

Just another scooter club from the north of England – but they were on the cusp of creating something big

Scooter racing may have been in their hearts, but the resurrection of the Lambretta Club Great Britain was what they were about to do

With plenty of accessories available, now was the time to put them all over a brand new Jet 200

Scooter gatherings were beginning to get bigger and bigger; something was starting to happen

Baitings Dam was a popular scooter race meeting and so it seemed for the crowds who gathered to watch

Scooters were beginning to catch the eye of the public wherever they went

Hydraulic disc brakes, expansion pipes, rev counters – taking Lambretta tuning to a new level

It wasn't just the Vespa and Lambretta scooters that could be converted for racing

Alan Smith flying the flag for both Britain and scooters

The game-changer

The Lambretta fire engine belonging to Mike Karslake – always on display to raise money for charity

Scooter boys 70s style

While the north may have been the epicentre of the scooter scene, things were beginning to hot up down south

No pub, it seemed, was safe from invasion

Now was the time to take scootering to the resorts

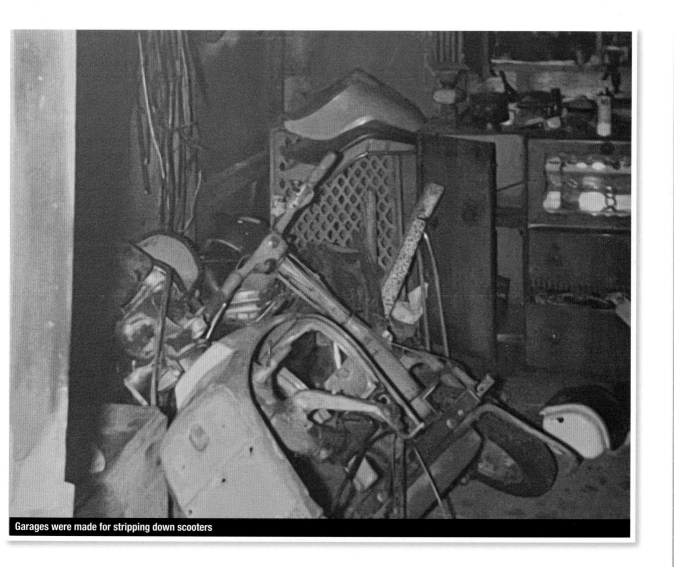

Garages were made for stripping down scooters

The typical scooterist back garden full of unwanted machines from the past, waiting for their resurrection

Magazine press shots couldn't help add motorcycles into the equation. Were they trying to stir something up?

Scootering was now about groups travelling around together. They say you are always safe in numbers

PEACEFUL MODS

More than 100 "mods" held a peaceful reunion in Brighton at the weekend to celebrate the tenth anniversary of the seaside mods and rockers riots of the sixties.

OWNERS NAME: *ROBIN GEORGE WILLIAMS*

REGISTRATION No: *AJT 935T*

EXPIRES ON: *17 · 4 · 79*

ENGINE No: *8446*

FRAME No: *58619*

CARD NUMBER: *2588*

Brighton was the place to be down south

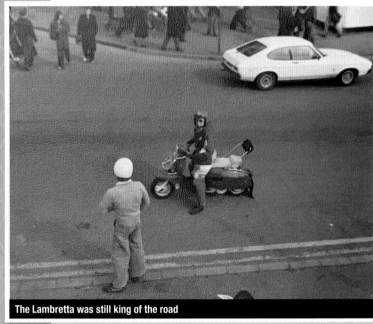
The Lambretta was still king of the road

It seemed all roads led up north and to one destination in particular

he media just couldn't forget the mods and rockers image, even by the late 1970s when such a distinction was increasingly meaningless

There was no doubt – the more you could bolt on the better it seemed your scooter would look

The chrome just got even bigger

They may have been a decade apart, but mods were on the rise once again

Soon the long hair and jeans would be gone as the scene started to change

ROADRATS – S.C.
JERSEY 'RUN' 1978 by
Lambretta

As the mod revival took hold it was easy to see how many young kids became engrossed; the L plates are clear evidence

The North may have been the mainstay of the 70s scooter scene, but the south made a huge contribution also

Dear Scooterist,

The Lambretta Club Great Britain is to be reformed as from 1st. January 1978. It will be run by m emb ers of Widnes Saints Scooter Club. Membership will run from January to December of each year. We beleive that there is a need for the club especially with the reintroduction of the GP150 and the GP200 next spring. The refreshing attitude toward Lambretta Scooters shown by the new Concessionaires points to a definite upsurge in the sales of new Lambrettas and hopefully this will lead to a healthy club m embership. This will help us to promote a varied programme of events and attractions.

The m em b ership fee has been fixed at £2 for individuals, and scooter clubs may affiliate to Lambretta Club for a fee of £1. Clubs affiliated to Lamb retta Club are au tomatically entered in the Overall Club Championship.

Southend 78 helped connect Lambretta and to a certain extent Vespa owners together. Mike Karslake was instrumental in making it happen and it was aimed at enthusiasts of all Innocenti creations

The new mod generation were happy to be part of it

Territories will always exist, so a club had to portray a show of strength

There was no doubt the Lambretta was the easier choice to customise and it was about to start happening on a national scale

Just being on a scooter was all that mattered, even in winter when the roads were at their most dangerous

Camping gear may have been basic by today's standards but it didn't matter as the era of rallies began to take shape

The open face helmet was standard
equipment for any scooterist

Also making a comeback – the sidecar

Coming soon to a layby near you…

…Or any back street

Jack and Madge pose with the combination of a soon to be famous scooter personality

Customisation is a personal thing, and some would lead by example

Terry Walton taking five minutes out from filming Quadrophenia on an old Vespa

QUADROPHENIA the Film

Quadrophenia is a film which shows how the mods rve revelled in pills, booze and aggro, but it also shows the comming down, the depression, the despair and the eventual suicide of the hero.

I am not going to go into the story itself, but there are one or two points which should be noted. Firstly when it showed mods arriving in Brighton, they were riding scooters, I didn't see one shot of mods arriving by bus, train or even in cars. Secondly that much of

Posing with others involved including Martyn 'Arthur' Scully at the front

he films success can be put down to the fact that they ed real mods as extras. No doubt they all have great raphbooks of momentoes but the one I like best is the ne of a well known mod from the Bolton area, sat in the ck of a police van wearing a greasy leather jacket, 's amazing what being broke can do to a man. If I am t mistaken the picture printed above, shows Phil from

The cast of extras for the film was made up of genuine scooterists, exactly how it should have been

WORLD GALA PREMIERE

QUADROPHENIA

Plaza 1, Lower Regent Street,
Thursday, 16th August 1979
7.15 pm for 8.00 pm

A 12

Black Tie

Brighton was seen as the epicentre of mod gatherings in the 1960s and was back in favour once again

60's MOD REVIVAL

SCOOTER CLUBS RUN

TO COINCIDE WITH THE RELEASE OF THE FILM 'QUADROPHENIA', IN THE SUMMER OF 1979.

TO : **BRIGHTON**

(HOME OF THE MODS)

ORGANISED BY THE ROADRATS S.C. OF SCUNTHORPE. ALL CLUBS AND SOLO RIDERS ARE WELCOME TO INCREASE THE TURNOUT. TO TAKE PLACE ON :

Friday, 18th to Sunday, 20th May

MEET ON BRIGHTON FRONT ON FRIDAY NIGHT OR EN ROUTE OR AT THE BERKELEY HOTEL, SCUNTHORPE EARLY O' FRIDAY MORNING. HOPE THIS RUN WILL BE PUBLICISED.

FOR FURTHER INFO' CONTACT 'BRAD' (N° 1) SCUN' 69479 OR SEE ANY ROADRATS SC MEMBER.

As coastal towns were invaded with scooters, onlookers would look on in bemusement

No, you're not seeing double – some custom scooter desig were replicated

Scooters were now starting to see great individuality in their paintwork...

...and their chrome

Even brand new Indian Lambrettas would be radically altered

Barely a year old, a brand new Vespa could be completely overhauled

While it wasn't exactly new for the Lambretta, the cutdown look was becoming very fashionable

The influence of a popular up and coming band was being felt

lambretta club GREAT BRITAIN
PROMOTE
SOUTHEND RALLY '79

at TWO TREE ISLAND, LEIGH·ON·SEA
AUGUST BANK HOLIDAY sat sun mon

GRASS TRACK RACING

FIELD EVENTS

CONCOURSE etc.

'ON·SITE' DANCES

FILM SHOWS

LIVE GROUP

POLICE DISPLAY

Prizes for best Mod club, chrome scoot,
IMPROVED CAMPING FACILITIES
Water, food and toilets on the site
All Scooterists are welcome
'ALL IN' £2 – MEMBERS LCGB £1·50

Southend 1979 may have started quietly enough, but it didn't end that way. No wonder the rules for the rally were rather crudely taped to the side of a car

Entertainment that weekend was supplied by a Lambretta Vega

And it all started so peacefully

Panel art was now beginning to tell a story

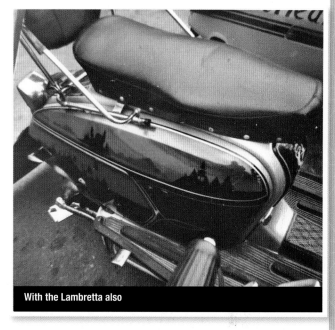

With the Lambretta also

Lens of Shipley was producing fine custom scooters in house

With the side panels removed the Lambretta was ideal for chroming

The front of a Vespa provided a huge canvas upon which to express yourself

Brass plating offered a different slant compared to chrome

Leopard skin print wasn't exclusive to ladies' fashion it seemed

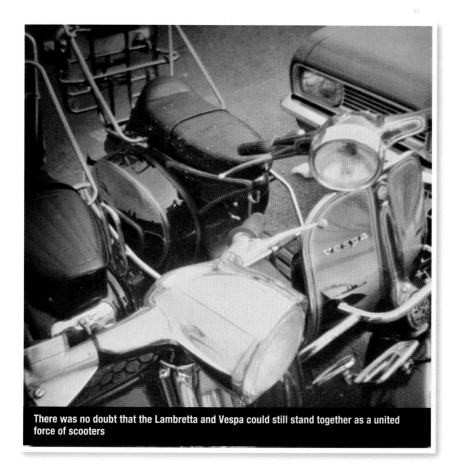

There was no doubt that the Lambretta and Vespa could still stand together as a united force of scooters

With Quadrophenia making a huge impact, seaside resorts were being swamped on holiday weekends

It would allow scooterists nationwide to congregate and unite as one

It wasn't just scooters that were customised, parkas were too

Northern destinations would become hugely popular

The atmosphere could be cut with a knife. There was bound to be a police presence, but it put everyone on edge

What did it matter? The younger generation enjoying themselves once again as the new trend gripped the nation

The scene was so vibrant, scooterists were keen to venture out in any weather…

...even in the midst of winter, regardless of how cold it was

As the decade finally came to an end Frank Osgerby was the fastest scooter man around

The AF 'S Type' – the must-have tuned Lambretta

The scene had even made its way to Ireland

The new generation of owners were the influencers. Perhaps the young lads on their bicycles would become the scooter boys of the 1980s